Gotthold Ephraim Lessing

The Education of the Human Race

Gotthold Ephraim Lessing

The Education of the Human Race

ISBN/EAN: 9783743305939

Manufactured in Europe, USA, Canada, Australia, Japa

Cover: Foto ©ninafisch / pixelio.de

Manufactured and distributed by brebook publishing software
(www.brebook.com)

Gotthold Ephraim Lessing

The Education of the Human Race

Preface.

I T is of some importance to understand rightly what principle really underlies the Divine Education of the Human Race, because we may be sure that such should be our rule in training and educating each Individual member.

Two ideas seem now in force; one a combination of Hope and Fear, by which fome teachers think it beft to educate—Fear of a Material Hell, Hope of a not much lefs Material Heaven. Thefe are the ultimates, up to which the leffer rewards and punifh-ments lead.

There is alfo the doctrine of the Divine Paternity of each individual foul, in virtue of which every member of the Race can be appealed to as a Child of God, and be urged to live as becomes fuch high relationfhip.

The writer of this Treatife thinks the latter is the true mode of dealing

with the fubject; and although he calls
not on any hafty traveller, who may be
impatient to reach his night quarters,
to turn afide from the eminence from
which he is gazing—yet he believes
that he fees fomewhat more than the
prefcribed road of his time: that he
fees fomewhat of the plan by which
the Race has hitherto been educated :
and he obtains, therefrom, fome hints
and fuggeftions as to its future deftiny.

He does not offer thefe thoughts as
the fum and fubftance of the matter,
but rather as fuggeftions tending towards the difcovery of fuller truth

through some other minds. And in this mood he seems to harmonize well with those who are expecting, not a *new* Revelation, but an ever-growing development of the *meaning* of that with which God has already furnished us: for assuredly we have not yet fathomed the infinite depths of the Divine Love for His Creatures. In our " Schemes of Redemption," and " Plans of Salvation," we have not yet reached the full meaning of that name under which God has revealed Himself in these latter days—OUR FATHER.

In our eagerness to prove the damnation of every foul who does not believe this or that dogma, we are in danger of forgetting that Chriftianity is either a Gofpel of Salvation, or is valuelefs: and we overlook the inevitable neceffity that the human mind muft pafs through phafes of ignorance, doubt, and even error, before it can become capable of receiving pure truth.

All the laws of the Univerfe have had exiftence from the beginning, yet how recently is it that Electricity has been difcovered? and do we yet know all which this power implies?

Did the earth ever do other than go round the fun? yet how long is it fince man found this out?

And are the fpiritual truths of man's nature more eafily difcerned than the phyfical phenomena which furround him? Why fhould there not be development in thefe as well as in thofe?

Each little fect or religion has, doubtlefs, had fome germ of the truth within it, which has rendered it fubfervient to the great purpofe of fertilizing the world—but fo long

as the profeffors of either of them
think that they are favoured Children
of the Divine Father, whom He regards with a complacency with which
He does not view the reft of
Humanity, fo long is the fulnefs of
God's idea not attained by them.

There may be much in this little
Treatife which will be perplexing to
men who merely read by the light
of eftablifhed and recognifed formulas;
much, which may found like herefy
to thofe who believe only that which
can be found to be contained within
the Articles and Creeds of their own

fchool; but to the honeft, earneft
Enquirer, it may fuggeft very profitable
currents of thought, in which he may
let his reafon and imagination flow
together, poffibly in one of thefe flow-
ing at laft into the great ocean of
Truth itfelf.

THE
EDUCATION
OF
THE HUMAN RACE.

I.

THAT which Education is to
the Individual, Revelation
is to the Race.

2.

EDUCATION is Revelation coming to
the Individual Man; and Revelation

1

B

is Education which has come, and is yet coming, to the Human Race.

3.

WHETHER it can be of any advantage to the fcience of inftruction to contemplate Education in this point of view, I will not here inquire; but in Theology it may unqueftionably be of great advantage, and may remove many difficulties, if Revelation be conceived of as the Educator of Humanity.

4.

EDUCATION gives to Man nothing which he might not educe out of himfelf; it gives him that which he might educe out of himfelf, only quicker and more eafily. In the fame way too, Revelation gives nothing to the human fpecies, which the human reafon left to itfelf might not attain; only it has given, and ftill gives to it, the moft important of thefe things earlier.

5.

AND juft as in Education, it is not a matter of indifference in what order the powers of a man are developed, as it cannot impart to a man all at once; fo was God alfo neceffitated to maintain a certain order, and a certain meafure in His Revelation.

6.

EVEN if the firft man were fur-nifhed at once with a conception of the One God; yet it was not poffible that this conception, imparted, and not gained by thought, fhould fubfift long in its clearnefs. As foon as the Human Reafon, left to itfelf, began to elaborate it, it broke up the one Immeafurable into many Meafurables, and gave a note or fign of mark to every one of thefe parts.

7.

HENCE naturally arofe polytheifm and idolatry. And who can fay how many millions of years human reafon would have been bewildered in thefe errors, even though in all places and times there were individual men who recognifed them *as* errors, had it not pleafed God to afford it a better direction by means of a new Impulfe?

8.

BUT when He neither could nor would reveal Himfelf any more to *each* individual man, He felected an individual People for His fpecial education; and that exactly the moſt rude and the moſt unruly, in order to begin with it from the very commencement.

9.

Tɪɪs was the Hebrew People, reſpecting whom we do not in the leaſt know what kind of Divine Worſhip they had in Egypt. For ſo deſpiſed a race of ſlaves was not permitted to take part in the worſhip of the Egyptians; and the God of their fathers was entirely unknown to them.

10.

It is poſſible that the Egyptians

had expreffly prohibited the Hebrews from having a God or Gods, perhaps they had forced upon them the belief that their defpifed race had no God, no Gods, that to have a God or Gods was the prerogative of the fuperior Egyptians only, and this may have been fo held in order to have the power of tyrannifing over them with a greater fhow of fairnefs. Do Chriftians even now do much better with their flaves?

11.

To this rude people God caufed Himfelf to be announced firft, fimply as "the God of their fathers," in order to make them acquainted and familiar with the idea of a God belonging to them alſo, and to begin with confidence in Him.

12.

THROUGH the miracles with which He led them out of Egypt, and planted them in Canaan, He teſtified of Himſelf to them as a God mightier than any other God.

13.

AND as He proceeded, demonſtrating Himſelf to be the Mightieſt of all, which only One can be, He gradually accuſtomed them thus to the idea of THE ONE.

14

BUT how far was this conception of The One, below the true tranſcendental conception of the One which Reaſon learnt to derive, ſo late with certainty, from the conception of the Infinite One?

15.

ALTHOUGH the beſt of the people were already more or leſs approaching the true conception of the One only, the people as a whole could not for a long time elevate themſelves to it.

And this was the fole true reafon why they fo often abandoned their one GOD, and expected to find the One, *i.e.*, as they meant, the Mightieft, in fome God or other, belonging to another people.

16.

BUT of what kind of moral education was a people fo raw, fo incapable of abftract thoughts, and fo entirely in their childhood capable? Of none other but fuch as is adapted to the age of children, an education by rewards and punifhments addreffed to the fenfes.

17.

HERE too Education and Revelation meet together. As yet God could give to His people no other religion, no other law than one through obedience to which they might hope to be happy, or through difobedience to which they muſt fear to be unhappy. For as yet their regards went no further than this earth. They knew of no immortality of the foul; they yearned after no life to come. But now to reveal thefe things to one whofe reafon had as yet ſo little growth, what would it have been but the fame fault in the Divine Rule as is committed by the fchoolmafter, who choofes to hurry his pupil too rapidly, and boaft of his progrefs, rather than thoroughly to ground him?

18.

BUT, it will be afked, to what purpofe was this education of fo rude a people, a people with whom God had to begin fo entirely from the beginning? I reply, in order that in the procefs of time He might employ particular members of this nation as the Teachers of other people. He was bringing up in them the future

Teachers of the human race. It was Jews who became their teachers, none but Jews; only men out of a people fo brought up, could be their teachers.

19.

FOR to proceed. When the Child by dint of blows and careffes had grown and was now come to years of underftanding, the Father fent it at once into foreign countries: and here it recognifed at once the Good which in its Father's houfe it had poffeffed, and not been confcious of.

20.

WHILE God guided His chofen

people through all the degrees of a childlike education, the other nations of the earth had gone on by the light of reafon. The moft part had remained far behind the chofen people. Only a few had got before them. And this too, takes place with children, who are allowed to grow up left to themfelves: many remain quite raw, fome educate themfelves even to an aftonifhing degree.

21.

BUT as thefe more fortunate few prove nothing againft the ufe and the neceffity of Education, fo the few heathen nations, who even appear to have made a ſtart in the knowledge of God before the choſen people, prove nothing againſt a Revelation. The Child of Education begins with ſlow yet ſure footſteps; it is late in overtaking many a more happily organiſed child of nature; but it *does* overtake it; and thenceforth can never be diſtanced by it again.

22.

SIMILARLY — Putting aſide the doctrine of the Unity of God, which in a way is found, and in a way is not found, in the books of the Old

Teftament—that the doctrine of immortality at leaft is not difcoverable
in it, is wholly foreign to it, that all
doctrine connected therewith of reward
and punifhment in a future life, proves
juft as little againft the Divine origin
of thefe books. Notwithftanding the
abfence of thefe doctrines the account
of miracles and prophecies may be
perfectly true. For let us fuppofe
that thefe doctrines were not only
wanting therein, but even that they
were not at all true; let us fuppofe
that for mankind all was over in this
life; would the Being of God be for
this reafon lefs demonftrated? Would

God be for this lefs at liberty, would it leſs become Him, to take immediate charge of the temporal fortunes of any people out of this perifhable race? The miracles which He performed for the Jews, the prophecies which He caufed to be recorded through them, were furely not for the few mortal Jews, in whofe time they had happened and been recorded: He had His intentions therein in reference to the whole Jewifh people, to the entire Human Race, which, perhaps, is deftined to remain on earth for ever, though every individual Jew and every individual man die for ever.

23.

ONCE more, The abfence of thofe doctrines in the writings of the Old Teftament proves nothing againft their Divinity. Mofes was fent from God even though the fanction of his law only extended to this life. For why fhould it extend further? He was furely fent only to the Ifraelitifh people, to the Ifraelitifh people *of that time*, and his commiffion was perfectly adapted to the knowledge, capacities, yearnings of the *then exift-ing* Ifraelitifh people, as well as to the deftination of that which belonged to the future. And this is fufficient.

24.

So far ought Warburton to have gone, and no further. But that learned man overdrew the bow. Not content that the abfence of thefe doctrines was no *dijcredit* to the Divine miffion of Mofes, it muft even be a *proof* to him of the Divinity of the miffion. And if he had only fought this proof in the adaptation of fuch a law to fuch a people!

But he betook himfelf to the hypothefis of a miraculous fyftem continued in an unbroken line from Mofes to Chrift, according to which, God had made every individual Jew exactly happy or unhappy, in proportion as his obedience or difobedience to the law deferved. He would have it that this miraculous fyftem had compenfated for the want of thofe doctrines (of eternal rewards and punifhments, &c.,) without which no ftate can fubfift; and that fuch a compenfation even proved what that want at firft fight appeared to negative.

25.

How well it was that Warburton could by no argument prove or even make likely this continuous miracle, in which he placed the exiftence of the Ifraelitifh Theocracy! For could he have done fo, in truth, he could then, and not till then, have made the difficulty really infuperable, to me at leaft. For that which was meant to prove the Divine character of the Miffion of Mofes, would have rendered the matter itfelf doubtful, which God, it is true, did not intend *then* to reveal; but which, on the other hand, He certainly would not render un-attainable.

26.

I EXPLAIN myfelf by that which is a picture of Revelation. A Primer for children may fairly pafs over in filence this or that important piece of the knowledge or art which it expounds, refpecting which the Teacher judged, that it is not yet fitted for the capacities of the children for whom he was writing. But it muft contain abfolutely nothing which blocks up the way towards the knowledge which is held back, or mifleads the children from it. Rather far, all the approaches towards it muft be carefully left open; and to lead them away from even one of thefe approaches, or to caufe them to enter it later than they need, would alone be enough to change the mere imperfection of fuch a Primer into an actual fault.

27.

In the fame way, in the writings of the Old Teftament thofe Primers for the rude Ifraelitifh people, un-practifed in thought, the doctrines of the immortality of the foul, and future recompenfes, might be fairly left out: but they were bound to contain nothing which could have even pro-craftinated the progrefs of the people, for whom they were written, in their way to this grand truth. And to fay but a fmall thing, what could have more procraſtinated it than the promiſe of ſuch a miraculous recompenſe in this life? A promiſe made by Him who promiſes nothing that He does not perform.

28.

FOR although in the unequal diſtribution of the goods of this life, Virtue and Vice ſeem to be taken little into conſideration, although this unequal diſtribution does not exactly afford a ſtrong proof of the immortality of the ſoul and of a life to come, in which this difficulty will be reſolved hereafter, it is certain that without this difficulty the human understanding would not for a long time, perhaps never, have arrived at better or firmer proofs. For what was to impel it to feek for thefe better proofs? Mere curiofity?

29.

An Ifraelite here and there, no doubt, might have extended to every individual member of the entire commonwealth, thofe promifes and threatenings which belonged to it as a whole, and be firmly perfuaded that whofoever fhould be pious muft alfo be happy, and that whoever was un-happy muft be bearing the penalty of his wrong-doing, which penalty would forthwith change itfelf into blefling, as foon as he abandoned his fin. Such a one appears to have written Job, for the plan of it is entirely in this fpirit.

30.

But daily experience could not poffibly be permitted to confirm this belief, or elfe it would have been all over, for ever, with the people who had this experience, fo far as all recognition and reception was concerned of the truth as yet unfamiliar to them. For if the pious were abfolutely happy, and it alfo of courfe was a neceffary

part of his happinefs that his fatisfaction fhould be broken by no uneafy
thoughts of death, and that he fhould
die old, and fatisfied with life to the
full : how could he yearn after another
life ? and how could he reflect upon a
thing after which he did not yearn ?
But if the pious did not reflect thereupon, who then fhould reflect ? The
tranfgreffor ? he who felt the punifhment of his mifdeeds, and if he curfed
this life muft have fo gladly renounced
that other exiflence ?

31.

MUCH lefs did it fignify if an

Ifraelite here and there directly and expreffly denied the immortality of the foul and future recompenfe, on account of the law having no reference thereto. The denial of an individual, had it even been a Solomon, did not arreft the progrefs of the general reafon, and was even in itfelf a proof that the nation had now come a great ftep nearer the truth. For individuals only deny what the many are bringing into confideration; and to bring into confideration that, concerning which no one troubled himfelf at all before, is half way to knowledge.

32.

LET us alfo acknowledge that it is a heroic obedience to obey the laws of God fimply becaufe they are God's laws, and not becaufe He has promifed to reward the obedience to them here and there ; to obey them even though there be an entire defpair of future recompenfe, and uncertainty refpecting a temporal one.

33.

MUST not a people educated in this heroic obedience towards God have been deflined, muft they not have been capable beyond all others of executing

Divine purpofes of quite a fpecial
character? Let the foldier, who pays
blind obedience to his leader, become
alfo convinced of his leader's wifdom,
and then fay what that leader may not
undertake to achieve with him.

34.

As yet the Jewifh people had reverenced in their Jehovah rather the
mightieft than the wifeft of all Gods;
as yet they had rather feared Him
as a jealous God than loved Him:
a proof this too, that the conceptions
which they had of their eternal One
God were not exactly the right con-

ceptions which we fhould have of God. However, now the time was come that thefe conceptions of theirs were to be expanded, ennobled, rectified, to accomplifh which God availed Himfelf of a quite natural means, a better and more correct meafure, by which it got the opportunity of appreciating Him.

35.

INSTEAD of, as hitherto, appreciating Him in contraft with the miferable idols of the fmall neighbouring peoples, with whom they lived in conftant rivalry, they began, in captivity under the wife Perfians, to meafure Him againft the " Being of all Beings " fuch as a more difciplined reafon recognifed and reverenced.

36.

REVELATION had guided their reafon, and now, all at once, reafon gave clearnefs to their Revelation.

37.

THIS was the firft reciprocal influence which thefe two (Reafon and Revelation) exercifed on one another; and fo far is the mutual influence from being unbecoming to the Author of them both, that without it either of them would have been ufelefs.

38.

THE child, fent abroad, faw other children who knew more, who lived more becomingly, and afked itfelf, in confufion, " Why do I not know that too? Why do I not live fo too? Ought I not to have been taught and admonifhed of all this in my Father's houfe?" Thereupon it again fought out its Primer, which had long been thrown into a corner, in order to throw off the blame upon the Primer. But behold, it difcovers that the blame does not reft upon the books, that the fhame is folely its own, for not having, long ago, known this very thing, and lived in this very way.

39.

SINCE the Jews, by this time, through the medium of the pure Perfian doctrine, recognifed in their Jehovah, not fimply the greateft of all national deities, but GOD; and fince they could the more readily find Him and indicate Him to others in their facred writings, inafmuch as He was really in them; and fince they manifefted as great an averfion for fenfuous reprefentations, or at all events were inftructed in thefe Scriptures, to have an averfion to them as great as the Perfians had always felt; what wonder that they found favour in the eyes of Cyrus, with a Divine Worfhip which he recognifed as being, no doubt, far below pure Sabeifm, but yet far above the rude idolatries which in its ftead had taken poffeffion of the forfaken land of the Jews.

40.

THUS enlightened refpecting the treafures which they had poffeffed without knowing it, they returned, and became quite another people. whofe firft care it was to give permanency to this illumination amongſt themſelves. Soon an apoſtacy and idolatry among them was out of the queſtion. For it is poſſible to be faithleſs to a national deity, but never to God, after He has once been recogniſed.

41.

THE theologians have tried to explain this complete change in the Jewiſh people in a different way ; and one, who has well demonſtrated the inſufficiency of theſe explanations, at laſt was for giving us, as the true account—" the vifible fulfilment of the prophecies which had been spoken and written refpecting the Babylonifh captivity and the reftoration from it." But even this reafon can be only fo far the true one, as it prefuppofes the, by this time, exalted ideas of God. The Jews muft by this time have recognifed that to do miracles, and to predict the future, belonged only to God, both of which they had afcribed formerly to falfe idols, by which it came to pafs that even miracles and prophecies had hitherto made fo weak an impreffion upon them.

42.

DOUBTLESS the Jews were made more acquainted with the doctrine of immortality among the Chaldeans and Perfians. They became more familiar with it too in the fchools of the Greek Philofophers in Egypt.

43.

HOWEVER, as this doctrine was not in the fame condition in reference to their Scriptures that the doctrine of God's Unity and Attributes were—fince the former were entirely overlooked by that fenfual people, while the latter would be fought for :—and fince too, for the former, previous exercifing was neceffary, and as yet there had been only *hints* and *allufions*, the faith in the immortality of the foul could naturally never be the faith of the entire people. It was and continued to be only the creed of a certain fection of them.

44.

AN example of what I mean by " previous exercifing" for the doctrine of immortality, is the Divine threatenings of punifhing the mifdeeds of the fathers upon the children unto the third and fourth generation.

This accuftomed the fathers to live in thought with their remoteft pof-terity, and to feel, as it were before-hand, the misfortune which they had brought upon thefe guiltlefs ones.

45.

By an allufion I mean that which was intended only to excite curiofity and to occafion queftions. As, for inftance, the oft-recurring mode of expreffion, defcribing death by " he was gathered to his fathers."

46.

By a " hint " I mean that which

already contains any germ, out of which the, as yet, held back truth allows itfelf to be developed. Of this character was the inference of Chrift from the naming of God "the God of Abraham, Ifaac, and Jacob." This hint appears to me to be un-queftionably capable of being worked out into a ftrong proof.

47.

IN fuch previous exercitations, allufions, hints, confifts the *pofitive* perfection of a Primer; juft as the above-mentioned peculiarity of not throwing difficulties or hindrances in the way to the fuppreffed truth, conftitutes the *negative* perfection of fuch a book.

48.

ADD to all this the clothing and the ftyle.

1. The clothing of abftract truths, which were not entirely to be passed over, in allegories and inftructive fingle circumftances, which were narrated as actual occurrences. Of this character are the Creation under the image of growing Day; the Origin of Evil in the ftory of the

Forbidden Tree; the fource of the variety of languages in the hiftory of the Tower of Babel, &c.

49.

2. THE ftyle—fometimes plain and fimple, fometimes poetical, through-out full of tautologies, but of fuch a kind as practife fagacity, fince they fometimes appear to be faying fome-thing elfe, and yet the fame thing; fometimes the fame thing over again, and yet to fignify or to be capable of fignifying, at the bottom, fomething elfe :—

50.

AND then you have all the properties of excellence which belong to a Primer for a childlike people, as well as for children.

51.

BUT every Primer is only for a certain age. To delay the child, that has outgrown it, longer in it than it was intended for, is hurtful. For to be able to do this in a way in any fort profitable, you muſt infert into it more than there is really in it, and extract from it more than it can contain. You muſt look for and

make too much of allufions and hints;
fqueeze allegories too clofely; inter-
pret examples too circumftantially;
prefs too much upon words. This
gives the child a petty, crooked,
hairfplitting underftanding: it makes
him full of myfteries, fuperftitions;
full of contempt for all that is com-
prehenfible and eafy.

52.

THE very way in which the Rab-
bins handled *their* facred books! The
very character which they thereby
imparted to the character of their
people!

53.

A BETTER Inſtructor muſt come and tear the exhauſted Primer from the child's hands. CHRIST came!

54.

THAT portion of the human race which God had willed to comprehend in one Educational plan, was ripe for the ſecond ſtep of Education. He had, however, only willed to comprehend on ſuch a plan, one which by language, mode of action, government, and other natural and political relationſhips, was already united in itſelf.

55.

THAT is, this portion of the human race was come fo far in the exercife of its reafon, as to need, and to be able to make ufe of, nobler and worthier motives of moral action than temporal rewards and punifhments, which had hitherto been its guides. The child had become a youth. Sweetmeats and toys have given place to the budding defire to be as free, as honoured, and as happy as its elder brother.

56.

FOR a long time, already, the beft

individuals of that portion of the human race (called above the eldeſt brother) had been accuſtomed to let themſelves be ruled by the ſhadow of ſuch nobler motives. The Greek and Roman did everything to live on after this life, even if it were only in the remembrance of their fellow-citizens.

57.

IT was time that another *true* life to be expected after this ſhould gain an influence over the youth's actions.

58.

AND fo Chrift was the firft certain practical Teacher of the immortality of the foul.

59.

THE firft *certain* Teacher. Certain, through the prophecies which were fulfilled in Him; certain, through the miracles which He achieved; certain, through His own revival after a death through which He had fealed His doctrine. Whether we can ftill *prove* this revival, thefe miracles, I put afide, as I leave on one fide *who* the Perfon of Chrift was. All *that* may have been at that time of great weight for the *reception* of His doctrine, but it is now no longer of the same importance for the recognition of the *truth* of His doctrine.

60.

THE first *practical* Teacher. For it is one thing to conjecture, to wish, and to believe the immortality of the soul, as a philosophic speculation: quite another thing to direct the inner and outer acts by it.

61.

AND this at least Christ was the

firft to teach. For although, already before Him, the belief had been introduced among many nations, that bad actions have yet to be punifhed in that life; yet they were only fuch actions as were injurious to civil fociety, and confequently, too, had already had their punifhment in civil fociety. To enforce an inward purity of heart in reference to another life, was referved for Him alone.

62.

His difciples have faithfully propagated thefe doctrines: and if they had even had no other merit, than that of

having effected a more general publi-
cation, among other nations, of a Truth
which Chrift had appeared to have
deftined only for the Jews, yet would
they have, even on that account alone,
to be reckoned among the Benefactors
and Fofterers of the Human Race.

63.

IF, however, they tranfplanted this
one great Truth together with other
doctrines, whofe truth was lefs en-
lightening, whofe ufefulnefs was of a
lefs exalted character, how could it be
otherwife? Let us not blame them
for this, but rather ferioufly examine

whether thefe very commingled doctrines have not become a new *impulfe*
of *direction* for human reafon.

64.

AT leaft, it is already clear that the
New Teftament Scriptures, in which
thefe doctrines after fome time were
found preferved, have afforded, and
still afford, the fecond better Primer
for the race of man.

65.

FOR feven hundred years paft they
have exercifed human reafon more

than all other books, and enlightened it more, were it even only through the light which the human reaſon itſelf threw into them.

66.

IT would have been impoſſible for any other book to become ſo generally known among different nations: and indiſputably, the fact that modes of thought ſo diverſe from each other have been occupied on the ſame book, has helped on the human reaſon more than if every nation had had its *own* Primer ſpecially for itſelf.

67.

IT was alſo highly neceſſary that each people for a period ſhould hold this Book as the *ne plus ultra* of their knowledge. For the youth muſt con-ſider his Primer as the firſt of all books, that the impatience to finiſh this book, may not hurry him on to things for which he has, as yet, laid no baſis.

68.

AND one thing is alſo of the greateſt importance even now. Thou abler ſpirit, who art fretting and reſtleſs over the last page of the Primer, beware!

Beware of letting thy weaker fellow-fcholars mark what thou perceiveft afar, or what thou art beginning to fee!

69.

Until thefe weaker fellow-fcholars are up with thee, rather return once more back into this Primer, and examine whether that which thou takeft only for duplicates of the method, for a blunder in the teaching, is not perhaps fomething more.

70.

Thou haft feen in the childhood of the human race, refpecting the doctrine of God's unity, that God makes immediate revelations of mere truths of reason, or has permitted and caused pure truths of reason to be taught, for some time, as truths of immediate revelation, in order to promulgate them the more rapidly, and ground them the more firmly.

71.

THOU experiencest in the boyhood of the Race the same thing in reference to the doctrine of the immortality of the soul. It is *preached* in the better Primer as a Revelation, instead of *taught* as a result of human reason.

72.

As we by this time can difpenfe with the Old Teftament, in reference to the doctrine of the unity of God, and as we are by degrees beginning alfo to be lefs dependent on the New Teftament, in reference to the immortality of the foul : might there not in this Book alfo be other truths of the fame fort prefigured, mirrored as it were, which we are to marvel at, as revelations, exactly fo long as until the time fhall come when Reafon fhall have learned to educe them, out of its other demonftrated truths, and bind them up with them?

73.

FOR inſtance, the doctrine of the
Trinity. How if this doctrine ſhould
at laſt, after endlefs errors, right and
left, only bring men on the road
to recogniſe that God cannot poſſibly
be One in the ſenſe in which finite
things are one, that even His unity
muſt be a tranſcendental unity, which
does not exclude a ſort of plurality?
Muſt not God at leaſt have the moſt
perfect conception of Himſelf, *i.e.,* a
conception in which is found every
thing which is in Him? But would
every thing be found in it which is in
Him, if a mere conception, a mere

poffibility, were found even of His neceffary Reality as well as of His other qualities? This poffibility exhaufts the being of His other qualities. Does it that of His neceffary Reality? I think not. Confequently God can either have no perfect conception of Himfelf at all, or this perfect conception is juft as neceffarily real, *i.e.,* actually exiftent, as He Himfelf is. Certainly the image of myfelf in the mirror is nothing but an empty reprefentation of me, becaufe it only has that of me upon the furface of which beams of light fall. But now if this image had everything, everything

without exception, which I have myfelf, would it then ftill be a mere
empty reprefentation, or not rather a
true reduplication of myfelf? When
I believe that I recognife in God a
fimilar reduplication, I perhaps do not
fo much err, as that my language is
infufficient for my ideas: and fo much
at leaft remains for ever incontrover-
tible, that they who wifh to make the
idea thereof popular for comprehen-
fion, could fcarcely have expreffed
themfelves more intelligibly and fuit-
ably than by giving the name of a
Son begotten from Eternity.

74.

AND the doctrine of Original Sin.
How, if at laft everything were to
convince us, that man ftanding on the
firft and loweft ftep of his humanity,
is not fo entirely mafter of his actions
as to be *able* to obey moral laws!

75.

AND the doctrine of the Son's
fatisfaction. How, if at laft, all com-
pelled us to affume that God, in fpite
of that original incapacity of man,
chofe rather to give him moral laws,
and forgive him all tranfgreffions in
confideration of His Son, *i.e.*, in con-

fideration of the felf-exiftent total of all His own perfections, compared with which, and in which, all imperfections of the individual difappear, than *not* to give him thofe laws, and then to exclude him from all moral bleffednefs, which cannot be conceived of without moral laws?

76.

LET it not be objected that fpeculations of this defcription upon the myfteries of religion are forbidden. The word myftery fignified, in the firft ages of Chriftianity, fomething quite different from what it means now: and the cultivation of revealed truths into truths of reafon, is abfolutely neceffary, if the human race is to be affifted by them. When they were revealed they were certainly no truths of reafon, but they were revealed in order to become fuch. They were like the " that makes "— of the ciphering mafter, which he fays to the boys, beforehand, in order to direct them, thereby in their reckoning. If the fcholars were to be fatisfied with the " that makes," they would never learn to calculate, and would fruftrate the intention with which their good mafter gave them a guiding clue in their work.

77.

AND why fhould not we too, by means of a religion whofe hiftorical truth, if you will, looks dubious, be conducted in a fimilar way to clofer and better conceptions of the Divine Being, our own nature, our relation to God, truths at which the human reafon would never have arrived of itfelf?

78.

IT is not true that fpeculations upon

thefe things have ever done harm or become injurious to the body politic. You muft reproach, not the fpeculations, but the folly and the tyranny of checking them. You muft lay the blame on thofe who would not permit men having their own fpeculations, to exercife them.

79.

ON the contrary, fpeculations of this fort, whatever the refult, are unqueftionably the moft fitting exercifes of the human heart, generally, fo long as the human heart, generally, is at

beft only capable of loving virtue for
the fake of its eternal bleffed con-
fequences.

80.

For in this felfifhnefs of the human
heart, to will to practife the underftanding too, only on that which
concerns our corporal needs, would be
to blunt rather than fharpen it. It
abfolutely *will* be exercifed on fpiritual
objects, if it is to attain its perfect
illumination, and bring out that purity
of heart which makes us capable of
loving virtue for its own fake alone.

81.

OR, is the human fpecies never to arrive at this higheft ftep of illumination and purity ?—Never ?

82.

NEVER ?—Let me not think this blafphemy, All Merciful! Education has its goal, in the Race, no lefs than in the Individual. That which is educated is educated for *fomething*.

83.

THE flattering profpects which are opened to the pupil, the Honour and Well-being which are painted to him, what are they more than means of educating him to become a man, who, when thefe profpects of Honour and Well-being have vanifhed, fhall be able to do his *Duty ?*

84.

THIS is the aim of *human* education, and fhould not the Divine education extend as far? Is that which is fuccefsful in the way of Art with the individual, not to be fuccefsful in the way of Nature with the whole? Blafphemy! Blafphemy!

85.

No! It will come! it will affuredly come! the time of the perfecting, when man, the more convinced his underftanding feels itfelf of an ever better Future, will neverthelefs not be neceffitated to borrow motives of action from this Future; for he will do the Right becaufe it *is* right, not becaufe arbitrary rewards are annexed thereto, which formerly were intended fimply to fix and ftrengthen his unfteady ga e in recognifing the inner, better, rewards of well-doing.

86.

It will affuredly come! the time of

a new eternal Gofpel, which is promifed us in the Primer of the New
Teftament itfelf!

87.

PERHAPS even fome enthufiafts of
the thirteenth and fourteenth centuries
had caught a glimpfe of a beam of
this new eternal Gofpel, and only erred
in that they predicted its outburft as
fo near to their own time.

88.

PERHAPS their " Three Ages of the
World" were not fo empty a fpecu-

lation after all, and affuredly they had
no contemptible views when they
taught that the New Covenant muft
become as much antiquated as the
Old has been. There remained by
them the fimilarity of the economy of
the fame God. Ever, to let them
fpeak my words, ever the felf-fame
plan of the Education of the Race.

89.

ONLY they were premature. Only
they believed that they could make
their contemporaries, who had fcarcely
outgrown their childhood, without

enlightenment, without preparation, men worthy of their *Third Age.*

90.

AND it was juft this which made them enthufiafts. The enthufiaft often cafts true glances into the future, but for this future he cannot wait. He wifhes this future accelerated, and accelerated through him. That for which Nature takes thoufands of years is to mature itfelf in the moment of his exiftence. For what pofleffion has he in it if that which he recognifes as the Beft does not become the beft in his life time? Does he come back? Does he expect to come back? Marvellous only that this enthufiaftic expectation does not become more the fafhion among enthufiafts.

91.

Go thine infcrutable way, Eternal Providence! Only let me not defpair in Thee becaufe of this infcrutablenefs. Let me not defpair in Thee, even if Thy fteps appear to me to be going back. It is not true that the fhorteft line is always ftraight.

92.

THOU haft on Thine Eternal Way

fo much to carry on together, fo much to do! fo many afide fteps to take! And what if it were as good as proved that the vaft flow wheel, which brings mankind nearer to this perfection is only put in motion by fmaller, fwifter wheels, each of which contributes its own individual unit thereto?

93.

IT is fo! The very fame Way by which the Race reaches its perfection, muft every individual man — one fooner, another later—have travelled over. Have travelled over in one and the fame life? Can he have been, in one and the felf-fame life, a fenfual Jew and a fpiritual Chriftian? Can he in the felf-fame life have overtaken both?

94

SURELY not that! But why fhould not every individual man have exifted more than once upon this World?

95.

Is this hypothefis fo laughable merely becaufe it is the oldeft? Becaufe the human underftanding, before the fophiftries of the Schools had diffipated and debilitated it, lighted upon it at once?

96.

WHY may not even I have already performed thofe fteps of my perfecting which bring to man only temporal punifhments and rewards.

97.

AND once more, why not another time all thofe fteps, to perform which the views of Eternal Rewards fo powerfully affift us?

98.

WHY fhould I not come back as often as I am capable of acquiring frefh knowledge, frefh expertnefs? Do I bring away fo much from once, that there is nothing to repay the trouble of coming back?

99.

Is this a reafon againft it? Or, becaufe I forget that I have been here already? Happy is it for me that I do forget. The recollection of my former condition would permit me to make only a bad ufe of the prefent.

And that which even I muſt forget *now*, is that neceſſarily forgotten for ever?

100.

Or is it a reaſon againſt the hypotheſis that ſo much time would have been loſt to me? Loſt?—And how much then ſhould I miſs?—Is not a whole Eternity mine?

THE END.